This journal belongs to:

Printed in Great Britain
by Amazon

87435138R00070